DATE	DESCRIPTION	AMOUNT

DATE	DESCRIPTION	AMOUNT

DATE	DESCRIPTION	AMOUNT

DATE	DESCRIPTION	AMOUNT

DATE	DESCRIPTION	AMOUNT

DATE	DESCRIPTION	AMOUNT

DATE	DESCRIPTION	AMOUNT

DATE	DESCRIPTION	AMOUNT

DATE	DESCRIPTION	AMOUNT

DATE	DESCRIPTION	AMOUNT

DATE	DESCRIPTION	AMOUNT

DATE	DESCRIPTION	AMOUNT

DATE	DESCRIPTION	AMOUNT

DATE	DESCRIPTION	AMOUNT

DATE	DESCRIPTION	AMOUNT

DATE	DESCRIPTION	AMOUNT

DATE	DESCRIPTION	AMOUNT

DATE	DESCRIPTION	AMOUNT

DATE	DESCRIPTION	AMOUNT

DATE	DESCRIPTION	AMOUNT

DATE	DESCRIPTION	AMOUNT

DATE	DESCRIPTION	AMOUNT

DATE	DESCRIPTION	AMOUNT

DATE	DESCRIPTION	AMOUNT

DATE	DESCRIPTION	AMOUNT

DATE	DESCRIPTION	AMOUNT

DATE	DESCRIPTION	AMOUNT

DATE	DESCRIPTION	AMOUNT

DATE	DESCRIPTION	AMOUNT

DATE	DESCRIPTION	AMOUNT

DATE	DESCRIPTION	AMOUNT

DATE	DESCRIPTION	AMOUNT

DATE	DESCRIPTION	AMOUNT

DATE	DESCRIPTION	AMOUNT

DATE	DESCRIPTION	AMOUNT

DATE	DESCRIPTION	AMOUNT

DATE	DESCRIPTION	AMOUNT

DATE	DESCRIPTION	AMOUNT

DATE	DESCRIPTION	AMOUNT

DATE	DESCRIPTION	AMOUNT

DATE	DESCRIPTION	AMOUNT

DATE	DESCRIPTION	AMOUNT

DATE	DESCRIPTION	AMOUNT

DATE	DESCRIPTION	AMOUNT

DATE	DESCRIPTION	AMOUNT

DATE	DESCRIPTION	AMOUNT

DATE	DESCRIPTION	AMOUNT

DATE	DESCRIPTION	AMOUNT

DATE	DESCRIPTION	AMOUNT

DATE	DESCRIPTION	AMOUNT

DATE	DESCRIPTION	AMOUNT

DATE	DESCRIPTION	AMOUNT

DATE	DESCRIPTION	AMOUNT

DATE	DESCRIPTION	AMOUNT

DATE	DESCRIPTION	AMOUNT

DATE	DESCRIPTION	AMOUNT

DATE	DESCRIPTION	AMOUNT

DATE	DESCRIPTION	AMOUNT

DATE	DESCRIPTION	AMOUNT

DATE	DESCRIPTION	AMOUNT

DATE	DESCRIPTION	AMOUNT

DATE	DESCRIPTION	AMOUNT

DATE	DESCRIPTION	AMOUNT

DATE	DESCRIPTION	AMOUNT

DATE	DESCRIPTION	AMOUNT

DATE	DESCRIPTION	AMOUNT

DATE	DESCRIPTION	AMOUNT

DATE	DESCRIPTION	AMOUNT

DATE	DESCRIPTION	AMOUNT

DATE	DESCRIPTION	AMOUNT

DATE	DESCRIPTION	AMOUNT

DATE	DESCRIPTION	AMOUNT

DATE	DESCRIPTION	AMOUNT

DATE	DESCRIPTION	AMOUNT

DATE	DESCRIPTION	AMOUNT

DATE	DESCRIPTION	AMOUNT

DATE	DESCRIPTION	AMOUNT

DATE	DESCRIPTION	AMOUNT

DATE	DESCRIPTION	AMOUNT

DATE	DESCRIPTION	AMOUNT

DATE	DESCRIPTION	AMOUNT

DATE	DESCRIPTION	AMOUNT

DATE	DESCRIPTION	AMOUNT

DATE	DESCRIPTION	AMOUNT

DATE	DESCRIPTION	AMOUNT

DATE	DESCRIPTION	AMOUNT

DATE	DESCRIPTION	AMOUNT

DATE	DESCRIPTION	AMOUNT

DATE	DESCRIPTION	AMOUNT

DATE	DESCRIPTION	AMOUNT

DATE	DESCRIPTION	AMOUNT

DATE	DESCRIPTION	AMOUNT

DATE	DESCRIPTION	AMOUNT

DATE	DESCRIPTION	AMOUNT

DATE	DESCRIPTION	AMOUNT

DATE	DESCRIPTION	AMOUNT

DATE	DESCRIPTION	AMOUNT

DATE	DESCRIPTION	AMOUNT

DATE	DESCRIPTION	AMOUNT

DATE	DESCRIPTION	AMOUNT